OUR SOLAR SYSTEM

Earth

BY DANA MEACHEN RAU

Content Adviser: Dr. Stanley P. Jones, Assistant Director, Washington, D.C., Operations, NASA Classroom of the Future

Science Adviser: Terrence E. Young Jr., M.Ed., M.L.S., Jefferson Parish (La.) Public Schools

Reading Adviser: Dr. Linda D. Labbo, Department of Reading Education, College of Education, The University of Georgia

COMPASS POINT BOOKS

MINNEAPOLIS, MINNESOTA

For Derek

Compass Point Books
3722 West 50th Street, #115
Minneapolis, MN 55410

Visit Compass Point Books on the Internet at *www.compasspointbooks.com*
or e-mail your request to *custserv@compasspointbooks.com*

Editors: E. Russell Primm and Emily J. Dolbear
Photo Researcher: Svetlana Zhurkina
Photo Selector: Dana Meachen Rau
Designer: The Design Lab
Illustrator: Graphicstock

Library of Congress Cataloging-in-Publication Data

Rau, Dana Meachen, 1971–
   Earth / by Dana Meachen Rau.
     v. cm. — (Our solar system)
   Includes index.
   Contents: Looking at Earth—Looking at the way Earth moves—Looking through Earth—
   Looking at Earth's surface—Looking around Earth—Looking at Earth from space—
   Looking to the future—An Earth flyby—The solar system—Glossary—Did you know?—
   Want to know more?
   ISBN 0-7565-0295-0 (hardcover)
   1. Earth—Juvenile literature. [1. Earth.] I. Title.
   QB631.4 .R38 2002
   525—dc21   2002003027

Table of Contents

Looking at Earth

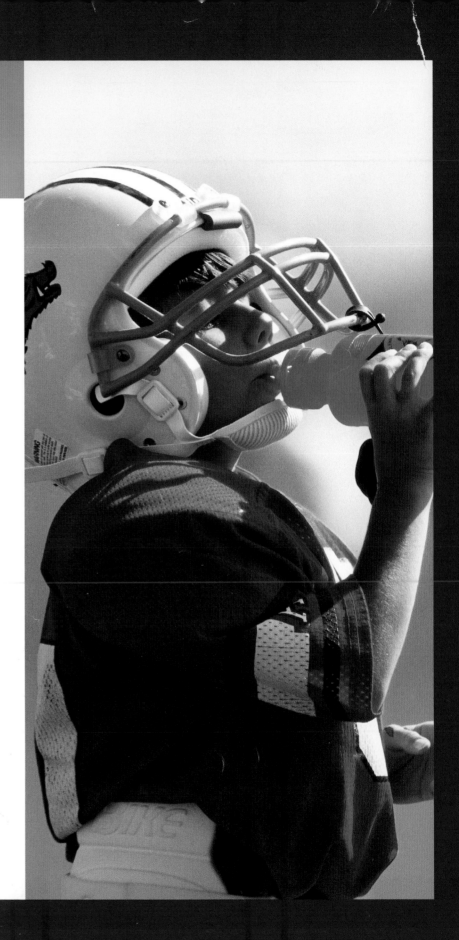

There is no place like home. Home has everything we need. It has a bed to sleep in. It has food to eat. It has books to read. It has a family to talk to. Earth is our home, too. Earth has everything we need to live. It has air for us to breathe. It has water for us to drink. And it has land for us to live on. We could not live on any other planet.

Earth is one of nine planets in the **solar system**. It is

Earth provides the water and food ▸ ▸▸
that people need to live.

the third planet from the Sun and the fifth-largest planet. We cannot look at Earth in the sky the way we look at the other planets. That's because we live on it.

Long ago, some people thought Earth was flat. Others believed it was round.

Finally, explorers sailed around Earth in their ships. They proved that Earth is a round globe. In the twentieth century, scientists finally saw its shape. They sent spacecraft into space to take pictures of the round ball of planet Earth.

In the sixteenth century, Polish **astronomer** Nicolaus Copernicus made an important discovery. At that time, people thought Earth was the center of the solar system. They believed that all the planets and the Sun orbited, or circled around, Earth. Copernicus studied the way the planets and the Sun move in the sky. He believed that the Sun was the center. He thought all the planets orbited around the Sun. Copernicus was right.

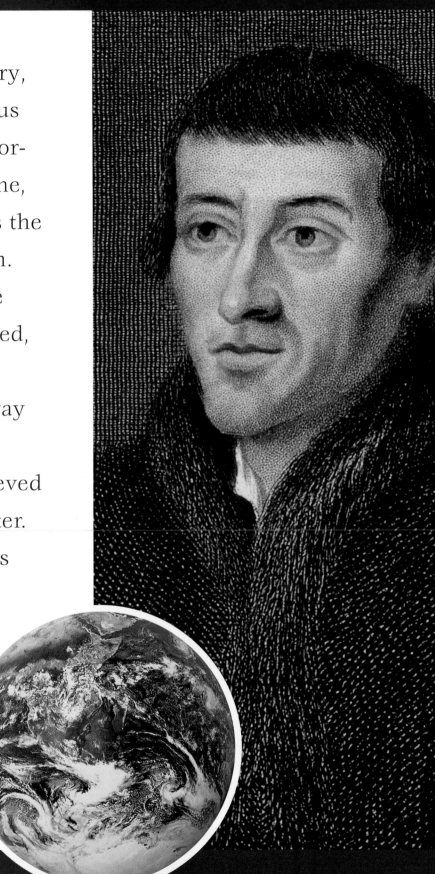

Nicolaus Copernicus ▶
(1473–1543) proved that the Sun was the center of the solar system.

People once thought Earth ▶
was flat. But Earth looks like a big ball floating in space.

Looking at the Way Earth Moves

✦ It doesn't feel like Earth is moving. But it is actually moving through space at about 67,000 miles (108,000 kilometers) per hour. It is traveling, or revolving, around the Sun in a path called an orbit. As it revolves, it is also spinning like a top. This spinning is called rotation.

Some of the Sun's light shines on Earth. It lights only half of Earth at a time. It is night on the dark side

◀ *Only half of Earth is lit by the Sun at a time. This creates day and night.*

and day on the light side. One rotation of Earth equals one day. Earth takes about twenty-four hours to spin once. On Earth, this spinning makes it look like the Sun is rising and setting in the sky. The daily rotation of Earth creates day and night. For thousands of years, this rotation has been the way for telling time.

It takes Earth about 365 days to travel around the Sun. One trip around the Sun is Earth's year. Earth's orbit is elliptical, or oval-shaped. Sometimes it is closer to the Sun than other times. Earth is also tilted slightly. The north pole is sometimes tipped closer to the Sun. Other times the south pole is closer. The elliptical orbit and the tilting create Earth's seasons.

The Sun appears to rise and set in the ▼
sky because Earth spins once a day.

Looking Through Earth

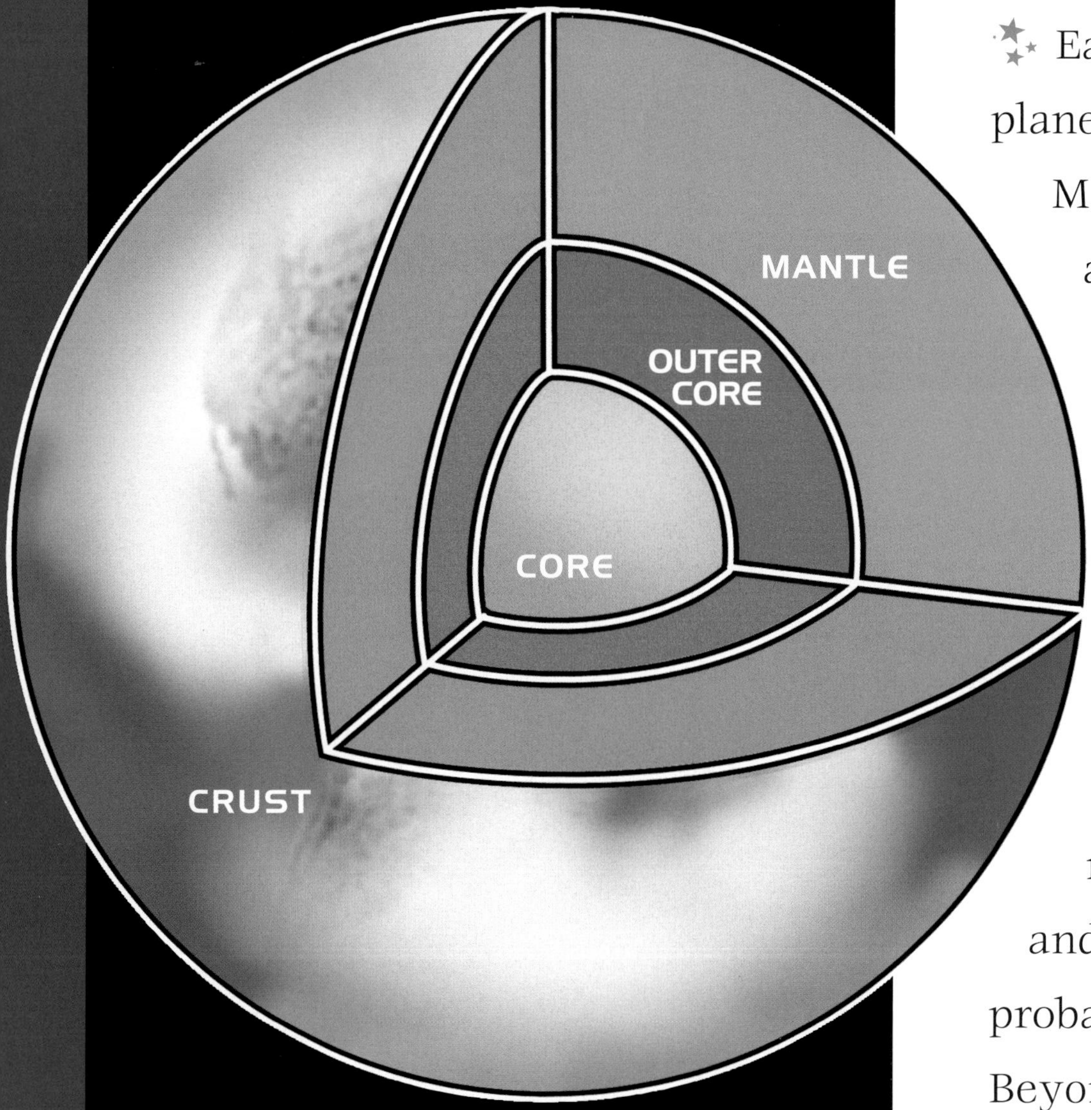

MANTLE

OUTER CORE

CORE

CRUST

Earth is one of the four planets made mostly of rock. Mercury, Venus, and Mars are the other rocky planets.

If you could cut Earth in half, you would see many layers. Deep in the center of Earth is a solid, round core. It is made of the metals iron and nickel. The core is hot, probably hotter than the Sun. Beyond the inner core is a liquid outer core. Next comes a large layer of thick, partly liquid rock called the **mantle**. Around the mantle is the crust. The crust is a thin layer of rock on the surface. The crust is usually thicker under land and thinner under oceans. Its thickness varies from about 4 to 25 miles (6 to 40 kilometers).

The other rocky planets also have crusts. But Earth's crust is different. It moves. The crust is made up of about thirty pieces called **tectonic plates**. These plates constantly shift around. Earthquakes occur when the plates move against one another or separate. Mountains are made when the plates crash into one

AMERICAN PLATE

PACIFIC PLATE

NAZCA PLATE

another. Volcanoes at the edges of plates shoot out a hot liquid rock called lava.

The layer of gases around Earth is called the atmosphere. It is made up of nitrogen, oxygen, and other gases needed for life. The atmosphere protects us from meteoroids. These are pieces of rock flying through space. Sometimes meteoroids hit planets. But most meteoroids burn up in Earth's atmosphere before they can reach the surface.

Earthquakes are caused by Earth's moving tectonic plates. ▲

Volcanoes erupt with hot liquid lava. ▶

Most meteoroids don't make it to Earth's surface. They burn up in the atmosphere and appear as shooting stars. ▶▶

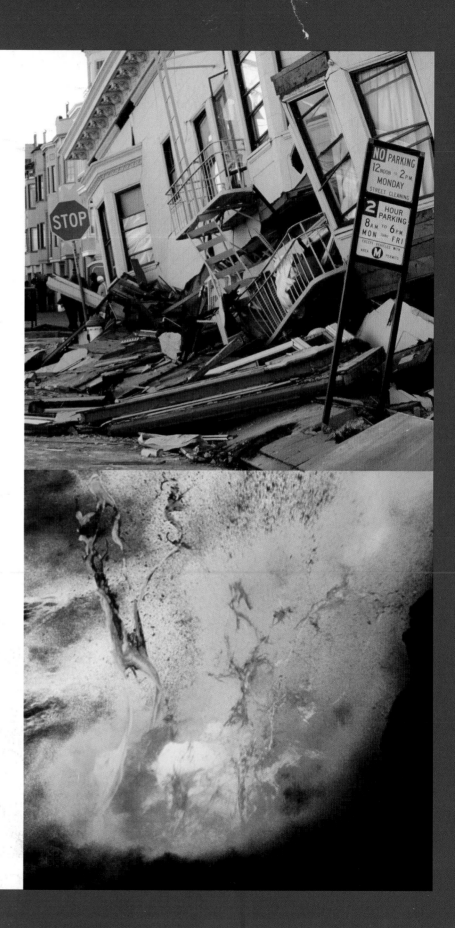

Looking at Earth's Surface

✨ From space, Earth looks like a blue ball with brown and green areas and swirling, white clouds. The blue color comes from something no other planet has—lots of water. More than two-thirds of Earth's surface is covered by water. This helps keep the temperature of Earth perfect for people to live, averaging about 72 degrees Fahrenheit (22 degrees Celsius).

On Earth, water takes the form of ▲ liquid (lake), solid (ice and snow), and gas (clouds).

Dry, sandy deserts are just one of many ▶ types of land found on Earth.

Water is found on Earth in three forms. It may be a solid, a liquid, and a gas. Solid water is called ice. Large areas of ice, or **ice caps**, are found at the poles. Water appears in its liquid form in Earth's oceans, lakes, and other bodies of water. Finally, water is found as a gas in the atmosphere.

The large brown and green land areas on Earth are called continents. Earth has seven continents. They are Africa, Antarctica, Asia, Australia, Europe, North America, and South America. The continents are covered with many different kinds of land. Earth has high mountains, dry deserts, thick forests, and cold ice.

The swirling, white clouds are in Earth's atmosphere. They create weather. Storms occur all over the planet.

The water, land, and sky of Earth are filled with many kinds of life. Millions of plants and animals live on Earth. Many types of people live on Earth, too.

This swirl of clouds is a large storm in ▶
Earth's atmosphere.

Many types of animals share the ▶▶
planet Earth.

Looking Around Earth

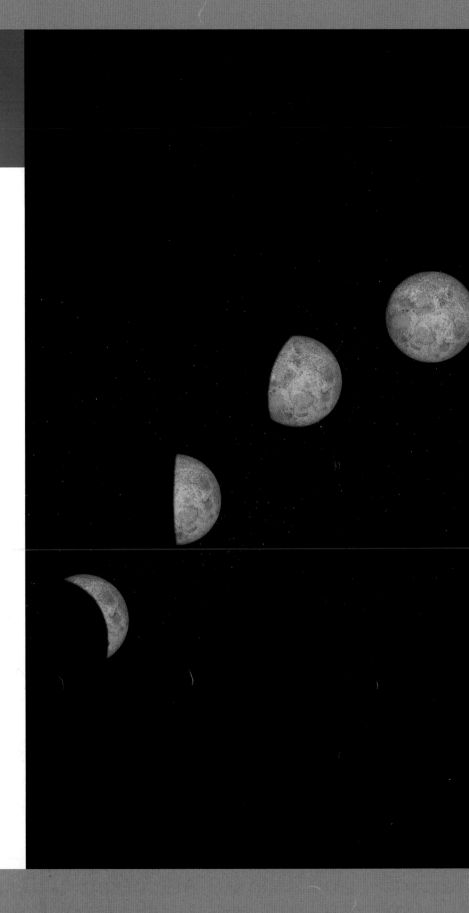

⁎ A satellite is an object that orbits a planet. The Earth has one natural satellite—the Moon. People have always known about the Moon. After the Sun, it is the second-brightest object in the sky.

The same side of the Moon always faces Earth. It is covered with many craters. The craters were formed by meteorites hitting the Moon's surface.

Scientists have ideas about how the Moon formed. They

The Moon's shape seems to change, ▶
depending on how much of the Moon's
bright side we can see from Earth.

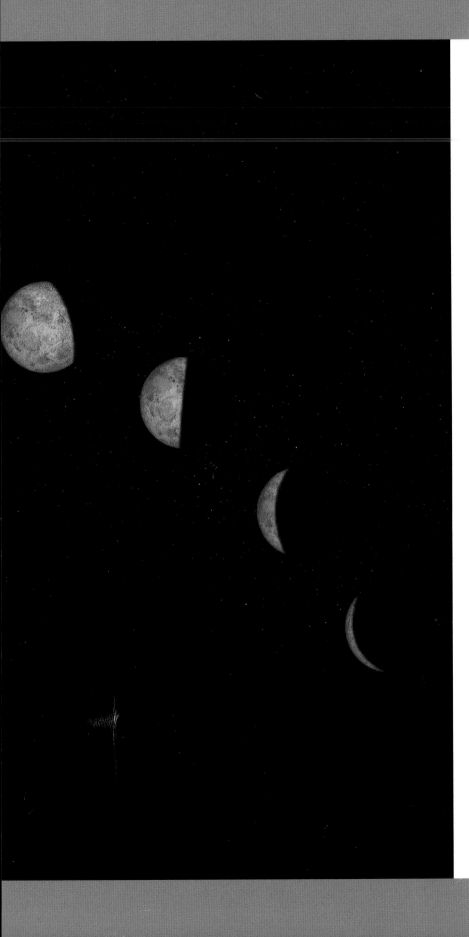

think Earth may have been
hit by another object long
ago. This caused pieces of
Earth to break off. These
pieces stayed in orbit around
Earth because of Earth's gravity. Gravity is the force that
pulls things toward the center
of Earth. Finally, these pieces
clumped up together and
formed the Moon.

From Earth, the Moon
looks as if it changes shape.
Sometimes we see a round
disk. Other times we see a
half-moon or crescent shape.
These different shapes are
called phases. From Earth,
the Moon looks like it goes
through phases because we

don't always see all of the side of the Moon that is lit by the Sun.

The Moon is the only object in the solar system—besides Earth, of course—that has been visited by people. In 1959, the Soviet Union (now Russia) sent *Luna 2* to the Moon. It was the first successful unmanned mission to the Moon. The United States sent many spacecraft to the Moon, too. After lots of training and practice, *Apollo 11* was sent to the Moon in 1969. On July 20, Neil Armstrong became the

Astronaut Buzz Aldrin walked on the ▲
Moon in 1969.

The Moon has a bumpy, uneven surface ▶
covered by craters.

first person to set foot on the Moon. Nineteen minutes after Armstrong, Buzz Aldrin joined him. They brought back samples of rocks for scientists on Earth to study.

People have not landed on the Moon since December 1972. Scientists have sent more spacecraft, though. *Clementine* in 1994 and the *Lunar Prospector* in 1998 mapped the surface of the Moon. They found water ice. The water lay inside deep craters at the Moon's poles, where it is hard for sunlight to reach.

Looking at Earth from Space

Scientists often send space-craft to other planets to learn more about them. But how do we find out more about our own planet?

The Moon is Earth's only natural satellite. But people have sent artificial, or human-made, satellites to orbit Earth. The first was called *Sputnik 1*. The Soviet Union launched it in 1959. On February 20, 1962, John Glenn Jr. became the first American to orbit Earth. He circled Earth three times. Since then, we have sent up thousands of satel-lites. Some satellites study clouds, temperature, and other weather patterns. Some collect facts about the oceans. The Landsat satellites watch the land. Some satellites help us communicate by phone, television, and computer.

Astronaut John Glenn Jr. was the first American to orbit Earth. His spacecraft was called Friendship 7.

Looking to the Future

✦ We live on Earth, but it is not easy to get information about our own planet. We can't go deep into Earth to study the core. We need spacecraft or satellites to see Earth from a distance. All we know for sure is what we can see on the surface.

Scientists believe that Earth formed about 4.5 billion years ago. We know Earth is changing all the time. People cause some of that change. Lights from big

◀ *Satellites orbit Earth and tell us more about the weather, land, and water of our planet.*

cities and plots of farmland can even be seen from space.

People have been burning coal, oil, and natural gas for centuries. These fuels are called fossil fuels. Carbon dioxide is one of the gases they release. This gas traps heat in Earth's atmosphere. This is making Earth slowly get warmer and warmer. This process is called the greenhouse effect. A greenhouse is a building that traps the Sun's heat inside it. Earth is becoming like a giant greenhouse.

We can learn a lot about Earth by looking ▶
all around us.

We must take care of our home planet. We must use land and water wisely and not destroy or waste them. We must also limit the burning of fossil fuels. We have to clean up the messes we have already made. Think of all the things you do to make your own home a nice place to live. We need to keep Earth just as nice for every person and every other living thing on the planet.

▼ *It is very important that people do their best to keep Earth a beautiful and safe place to live.*

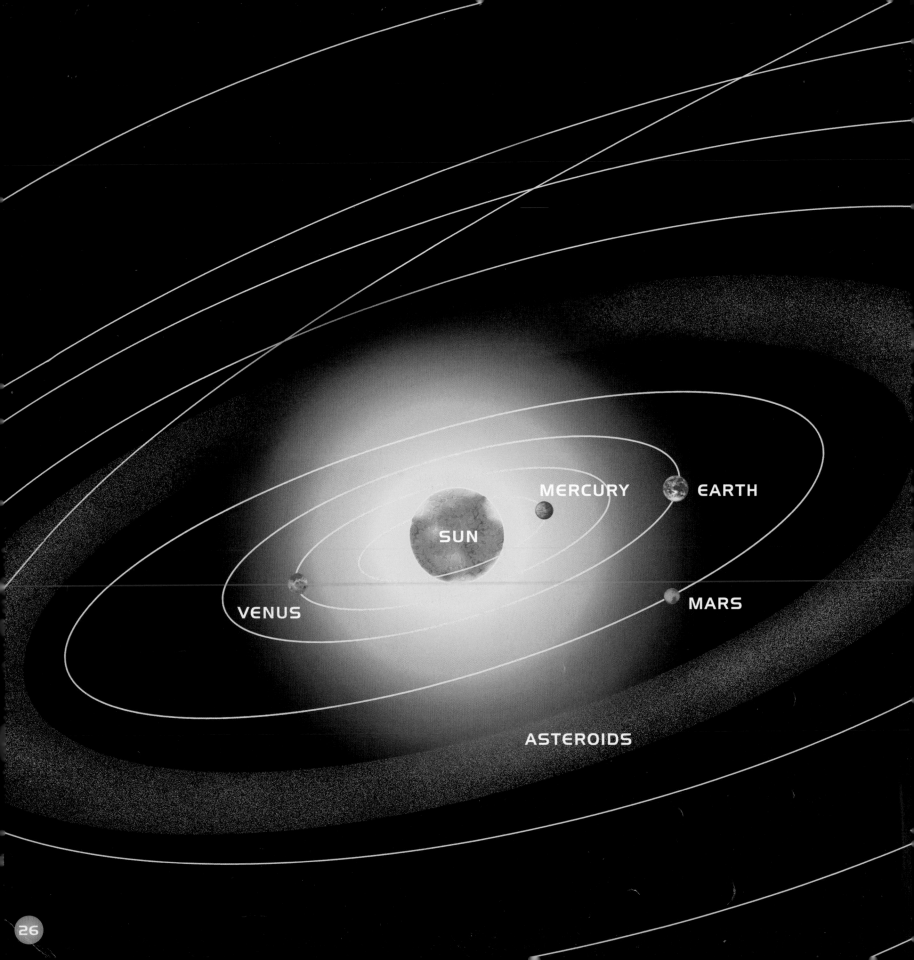

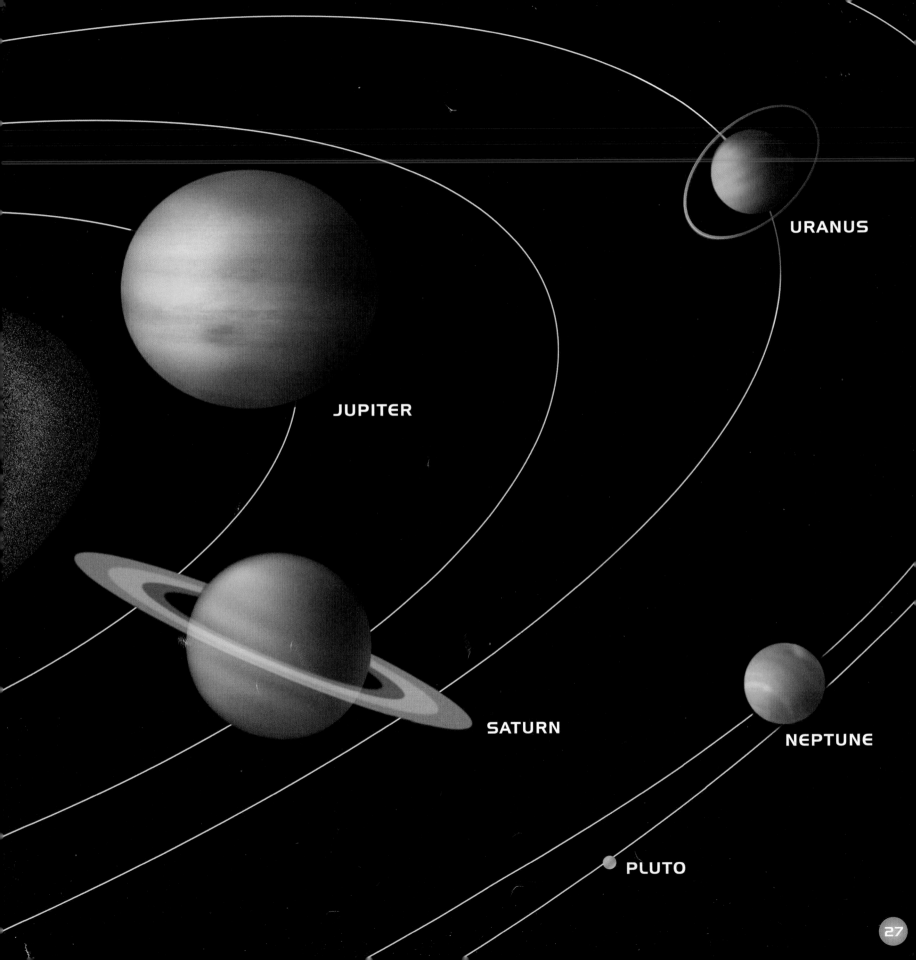

JUPITER

URANUS

SATURN

NEPTUNE

PLUTO

Glossary

astronomer—someone who studies space

core—the center of a planet

craters—bowl-shaped landforms created by meteorites crashing into a planet

ice caps—covers of ice and snow

mantle—a layer inside a planet often made of hot liquid

meteoroids—chunks of rock in space; when one hits a planet, it is called a meteorite

solar system—a group of objects in space including the Sun, planets, moons, asteroids, comets, and meteoroids

tectonic plates—moving pieces of the Earth's crust

pole—the northernmost or southernmost point on a planet

volcanoes—mountains that may erupt with hot liquid rock

An Earth Flyby

Earth is the fifth-largest planet and the third planet from the Sun.

Average distance from the Sun: 93 million miles (150 million kilometers)

Diameter: 7,926 miles (12,753 kilometers)

Time it takes to orbit around Sun (one year): 365 days and 6 hours

Time it takes to rotate (one day): 23 hours and 56 minutes

Structure: inner core, outer core, mantle, and crust

Did You Know?

- The Ring of Fire is an area around the Pacific basin. Many of the world's volcanoes are in this area.

- The Nile River in Egypt is the longest river on Earth. It is 4,145 miles (6,669 kilometers) long.

- The Grand Canyon in Arizona is the deepest canyon on Earth. It is more than 1 mile (1.6 kilometers) deep.

- Mount Everest in Asia is the highest point on Earth. It is 29,028 feet (8,854 meters) high.

- The Romans called the Moon *Luna*.

- About once a month, the Moon goes through a full cycle of phases. The word *month* comes from the word *moon*.

- The pull of the Moon's gravity is the main cause of tides on Earth. The tide is the rise and fall of the large bodies of water on Earth.

- Is it possible to live on the Moon? It might be possible if we could use the water found at the Moon's poles.

- Twelve men from the United States have walked on the Moon's surface.

- In the future, some people may live in space stations orbiting Earth. The International Space Station is being built right now.

- In 1961, Yuri Gagarin of the Soviet Union became the first human to orbit Earth. He died in a plane crash in 1968.

Average surface temperature: 72° Fahrenheit (22° Celsius)

Atmosphere: 77% nitrogen
21% oxygen
2% argon, carbon dioxide, water, and other gases

Atmospheric pressure: 1.0

Moons: 1

Rings: 0

Want to Know More?

AT THE LIBRARY

Gibbons, Gail. *Planet Earth: Inside Out*. New York: Mulberry Books, 1998.

Green, Jen. *Race to the Moon: The Story of Apollo 11*. Danbury, Conn.: Franklin Watts, 1998.

Landau, Elaine. *Earth Day: Keeping Our Planet Clean*. Springfield, N.J.: Enslow, 2002.

Lauber, Patricia. *You're Aboard Spaceship Earth*. New York: HarperTrophy, 1996.

Mitton, Jacqueline, and Simon Mitton. *Scholastic Encyclopedia of Space*. New York: Scholastic Reference, 1998.

ON THE WEB

Destination: Earth
http://earth.nasa.gov
The official web site of NASA's Earth science studies

Earth from Space
http://earth.jsc.nasa.gov/
For a collection of pictures of Earth taken from space

Exploring the Planets: Earth
http://www.nasm.edu/ceps/etp/earth/
For more information about Earth

The Nine Planets: Earth
http://www.seds.org/nineplanets/ nineplanets/earth.html
For a multimedia tour of Earth

Solar System Exploration: Earth
http://sse.jpl.nasa.gov/features/planets/ earth/earth.html
For more information about Earth and links to other Earth sites

Space Kids
http://spacekids.hq.nasa.gov
NASA's space science site designed for kids

Space.com
http://www.space.com
NASA's space science site designed for kids

Star Date Online: Earth
http://www.stardate.org/resources/ssguide/ earth.html
For an overview of Earth

Welcome to the Planets: Earth
http://pds.jpl.nasa.gov/planets/choices/ earth1.htm
For pictures and information about Earth and some of its most important surface features

THROUGH THE MAIL

Goddard Space Flight Center
Code 130, Public Affairs Office
Greenbelt, MD 20771
To learn more about space exploration

Jet Propulsion Laboratory
4800 Oak Grove Drive
Pasadena, CA 91109
To learn more about the spacecraft
missions

Lunar and Planetary Institute
3600 Bay Area Boulevard
Houston, TX 77058
To learn more about Earth and
other planets

Space Science Division
NASA Ames Research Center
Moffet Field, CA 94035
To learn more about Earth and
solar system exploration

ON THE ROAD

**Adler Planetarium and
Astronomy Museum**
1300 S. Lake Shore Drive
Chicago, IL 60605-2403
312/922-STAR
To visit the oldest planetarium
in the Western Hemisphere

***Exploring the Planets* and
*Where Next Columbus?***
National Air and Space Museum
7th and Independence Avenue, S.W.
Washington, DC 20560
202/357-2700
To learn more about the solar system
at this museum exhibit

**Rose Center for Earth and
Space/Hayden Planetarium**
Central Park West at 79th Street
New York, NY 10024-5192
212/769-5100
To visit this new planetarium and
learn more about the planets

UCO/Lick Observatory
University of California
Santa Cruz, CA 95064
408/274-5061
To see the telescope that was used to
discover the first planets outside of
our solar system

Index

◀ **About the Author:** *Dana Meachen Rau loves to study space. Her office walls are covered with pictures of planets, astronauts, and spacecraft. She also likes to look up at the sky with her telescope and write poems about what she sees. Ms. Rau is the author of more than seventy-five books for children, including nonfiction, biographies, storybooks, and early readers. She lives in Burlington, Connecticut, with her husband, Chris, and children, Charlie and Allison.*